FROM THE PULPIT

TO

PERDITION

BY

HENRY CLAY MORRISON

First Fruits Press
Wilmore, Kentucky
c2013

ISBN: 9781621710547 (Print), 9781621711414 (Digital)

From the Pulpit to Perdition by H.C. Morrison
First Fruits Press, © 2014
Previously published by the Pentecostal Publishing Company, circa 1920

Digital version at
http://place.asburyseminary.edu/firstfruitsheritagematerial/76/

First Fruits Press is a digital imprint of the Asbury Theological Seminary, B.L. Fisher Library. Asbury Theological Seminary is the legal owner of the material previously published by the Pentecostal Publishing Co. and reserves the right to release new editions of this material as well as new material produced by Asbury Theological Seminary. Its publications are available for noncommercial and educational uses, such as research, teaching and private study. First Fruits Press has licensed the digital version of this work under the Creative Commons Attribution Noncommercial 3.0 United States License. To view a copy of this license, visit http://creativecommons.org/licenses/by-nc/3.0/us/.

For all other uses, contact:

First Fruits Press
B.L. Fisher Library
Asbury Theological Seminary
204 N. Lexington Ave.
Wilmore, KY 40390
http://place.asburyseminary.edu/firstfruits

Morrison, H. C. (Henry Clay), 1857-1942.
   From the pulpit to perdition / by Henry Clay Morrison.
   32 p. : 21 cm
   Wilmore, Ky. : First Fruits Press, c2013.
   Reprint. Previously published: Louisville, Ky. : Pentecostal Pub. Co., [192-?].
   ISBN: 9781621710547 (pbk.)
   I. Title.
  PR409 .R4 M6 2014

Cover design by Haley Hill

asburyseminary.edu
800.2ASBURY
204 North Lexington Avenue
Wilmore, Kentucky 40390

FROM THE PULPIT
TO
PERDITION

PENTECOSTAL PUBLISHING COMPANY
Box 774, Louisville 1, Kentucky.

CONTENTS

Chapter	Page
1. Dr. Star And The White Temple	4
2. The Church Entertainment	.10
3. The Cyclone	.14
4. The Ascension	.16
5. Standing At Heaven's Gate	.21

CHAPTER I

DR. STAR AND THE WHITE TEMPLE

Rev. Clarence Jordan Star, D.D., was a man of fine physical proportions, with natural mental endowments far above the average man. His school advantages had been of the best, beginning with excellent teachers in his early childhood and graduating at one of the leading universities of the country. He had, in addition to this, taken a three years' course in a school of theology, gone well over the field literature, and traveled much abroad.

His social qualities were of a high order. With striking face, elegant, easy manners, and affable disposition, he won friends and admirers everywhere. He entered the work of the ministry under the most auspicious circumstances, and his rise was so rapid that within a few years from the time that he entered upon the duties of the pastorate, he was occupying one of the most important pulpits in the denomination to which he belonged. The Doctor was the personification of grace in the pulpit, and withal an eloquent speaker.

He enjoyed the reputation of being a liberal man, broad-minded, and tender-hearted. He was a popular man for occasions. If the corner-stone of a church was to be laid, or a monument to the memory of dead heroes to be unveiled, or the funeral of some prominent business man to be preached, Dr. Star was sought out for the service. The young people, not only of his congregation, but of the city generally, desired his presence and services on wedding occasions. Banquets and feasts seemed incomplete if Dr. Star did not say grace before the feast was served.

The church in which Dr. Star's congregation worshipped was in every sense worthy of such a pastor. It was a massive stone structure, with tall steeple and gorgeous windows. The interior was finished in hardwood, and the floor was covered with Brussels carpet. The pulpit was an elegant piece of elaborately carved mahogany, covered in front with red plush velvet, and decorated with a beautiful white silk cross. The baptismal font was of whitest marble; in fact everything in and about the church gave evidence of most refined taste and largest wealth. The church was called "The White Temple." The membership numbered about thirteen hundred, and was made up of merchants, manufacturers, bankers, and the first men of the learned professions of the city, with their families.

White Temple Church was a great center of fashion on the Sabbath, and of social life during the week days. In fact it had become, with its splendid festivals and beautiful entertainments, almost a rival of the theaters of the city. Besides the vast auditorium this church had lecture-rooms, sewing-rooms, dining-rooms, an immense kitchen, a reading-room and beautiful parlors.

The eloquence of Dr. Star, the fine music of his choir, with its variety of instruments, and its hired singers with trained voices, drew great congregations to The White Temple.

There was an unwritten, but perfectly well understood law, that drew the social lines closely between the masses and the classes, and The White Temple was the church of the classes. Dr. Star was not a sensational preacher—he was too cultivated a man for that. His drift was in the direction of higher criticism, his tastes were aesthetical, he believed in the highest mental culture for the mind both of men and women, and had in his church both Chautauqua Circles and Shakesperean Clubs. The Doctor's salary was large, and he was in demand as a lecturer at the great summer gatherings where his services commanded substantial pecuniary remuneration, and thus it was possible for his family to live, both in table and apparel, as well as the most wealthy of his parishioners.

The church and its pastor were thoroughly opposed to revivals of religion. The method of increasing the membership of the church was to take in the children of the various families as they arrived at the proper age, and if persons of proper social standing were found, whom it was thought desirable to bring into the membership of White Temple, social influences were shrewdly brought

FROM THE PULPIT TO PERDITION 7

to bear that generally resulted satisfactorily.

At the time of which I write there had, for sometime, been a sort of lull in the social life of this great church, and the leaders of the hosts had become aware of the fact that a revival of church enthusiasm and social life was necessary. With this end in view a meeting was called, and a movement set on foot to give an entertainment at The White Temple which should eclipse anything of the sort ever before undertaken by that congregation. That time might be ample for full preparation for the cantata and festival, the great event was fixed on a date many weeks away from the time of the committee meeting, and now the whole congregation was astir, and excitement and expectation were in due time brought to fever heat.

The proper persons were selected and carefully trained for the various parts in the play, and others were selected to keep stalls, and others to wait on the table at the sumptuous luncheon that was to be served.

Handsome and gay costumes were made, and there was no sparing of money or pains in the preparation for the coming event of the season in the great society circles that revolved about White Temple as its common center.

I must call the reader's attention to the fact that some years before the entertainment of which I write took place, a "Prophetic Convention" had been held in the city where this great church was located, in which the doctrines of entire sanctification and the second coming of Christ had been discussed. The discussion of these subjects had attracted much attention at the time. As one result of the convention several revivals had broken out and spread from place to place, resulting in a great awakening in many parts of the city, in which quite a number of the smaller congregations had participated, many hundreds of persons sought forgiveness of sins, and some scores professed full salvation.

Every church in the city felt, to a greater or less extent, the effect of these meetings. Even fashionable White Temple did not escape. Some of the congregation being greatly troubled at the thought of Christ's coming, and not a few of them much disturbed at the thought of holiness being necessary in order to escape the pit of outer darkness, it became necessary for Dr. Star to preach a series of sermons on the subjects discussed by the convention in order to quiet the fears of his people, and get them restored again to the even tenor of their ways.

I cannot here go into a detailed account of this series of sermons, or even undertake a systematic synopsis of them. It will suffice to say that Dr. Star followed the well-beaten track made by those who have gone before him, but it must be granted that he handled the subjects in a brilliant and striking way. He warned the people against fanaticism and narrow views of truth. He severely censured all sorts of religious excitement; he pointed out the hobby-rider and held him up to ridicule. He struck straight out from the shoulder at star gazers, who perverted the Scriptures on the subject of the second coming, and comforted his people by assuring them that time was yet in the early morning, with a vast sweep of centuries to roll by in an ever increasing development and culture of the race.

He said that only cranks and narrow-minded persons profess to be sanctified from all sin. He called their attention to the fact that Paul called himself the chief of sinners, and that John wrote, "If we say we have no sin we deceive ourselves and the truth is not in us."

For some four Sabbaths in succession Dr. Star strove to comfort the disturbed consciences among his people, assuring them that all men sin every day, and that we need not hope for or expect anything else. These sermons had the desired effect, and the Doctor soon saw, with much satisfaction, that the agitation in his church on the subject of the second coming, and sanctification, was entirely dissipated, and his gay and thoughtless people went forward with dancing parties, theaters, cards, and church festivals, with as much enthusiasm as they did before the great awakening visited the city.

CHAPTER II

THE CHURCH ENTERTAINMENT

The time for the greatest entertainment that White Temple had ever undertaken came at last. So many tickets had been sold that the idea of giving the entertainment in the lecture-room had to be given up, and the great auditorium was opened, and a stage, with a drop-curtain and beautiful scenery, was erected on the pulpit platform. Extra seats were improvised, chairs were placed in the aisles, and every seat in the vast auditorium was occupied, while men and boys stood about the doors, or sat upon the window sills. A band of music enlivened the hour in which the people gathered. There was hurrying to and fro as car after car landed at the door the beautiful maidens, arrayed in silks and satins, and bedecked with flowers, who were to take part in the entertainment.

The great city had rarely witnessed a more splendid gathering of wealth and beauty than assembled at White Temple on that memorable evening. Millionaires were there with their proud wives leaning on their arms, and their charming daughters upon the stage, and their stately sons participating in the festivities.

A thousand electric lights shed a light as bright as noon day upon the dazzling scene.

Dr. Star was present in elaborate clergyman's

coat, white tie, tall silk hat, and kid gloves. If ever a pastor looked with content and satisfaction over his flock, that man was Dr. Star, as his eye swept over the magnificent audience before him that night.

When everything was ready for the beginning of the play to be enacted upon the stage, a cornet sounded and the curtain rolled slowly up, revealing Dr. Star, standing like a piece of statuary in the center of the stage, surrounded by fifty beautiful maidens, all arrayed in spotless white. The Doctor stepped gracefully forward, and in a few well-chosen words welcomed the audience to the entertainment. He explained that recreation was better than medicine, that "religion never was designed to make our pleasures less." He congratulated himself that he was pastor of such a congregation of people, where large views and liberal actions had taken the place of superstition not worthy of the dark ages, yet to be found among the illiterate masses.

He closed his remarks with an eloquent tribute to the progress of science. As the curtain went down there was a great clapping of hands, and not a few persons who had brought flowers for their friends, in their enthusiasm threw them at their pastor's feet.

"What a divine man," whispered a wealthy sister, sitting on the front pew. As Dr. Star came down from the platform to take a prominent seat reserved for him, the people cheered again. All those within easy reach clasped his hand, and others nodded and smiled their approval.

The Doctor sat down as contented and happy as a man could well hope to be. Why not? No man ministered to a more cultured people, his salary was ample; his congregation filled all available space in his church; the papers were full of his praise; the products of his pen were sought by the leading publishers of the country. The Doctor himself, could hardly see how his surroundings could be improved.

The play went forward. The beautiful women and gallant men appeared in costumes appropriate to the parts they performed. There was no lack of talent, and the acting was more like that of noted stars than of amateurs.

When the curtain finally fell after the last scene, Dr. Star arose and announced that supper would be served to the members of the congregation in the basement below, and he hoped every one of his people would remain. Entreaty was unnecessary. Every stairway to the basement of the church was jammed with a merry throng of people.

Long tables were set in Sabbath-school and lecture-rooms, and tables in the sewing-rooms, and tables in the parlors, tables in nooks and corners, tables everywhere, where space could be found for a table that would accommodate even two persons. These tables were loaded with the fat of the

FROM THE PULPIT TO PERDITION 13

land. The sea had contributed of its treasures of shell-fish. There were roast pigs and turkeys and smaller fowls. Great vases of white brittle celery stood in long lines down every festal board. The finest breads that could be baked were heaped up in abundance. Delicious fruits from sunny climes, in cut-glass bowls, decorated every table; nuts and candies of every kind abounded, and flowers of every color were in lavish profusion. It was a feast of millionaires and merchant princes. The scene was rich and brilliant and gay beyond the powers of my pen to describe. The people sat down to eat. There were seven hundred seated at the tables, and three hundred waitresses in their white costumes, that showed the rosy tint of round, plump arms, served in the lighter work, while colored servants and strong young men bore the burden of the task.

The social revival had reached high tide at White Temple. A delirium of delight and gaiety seemed to pervade the place, and all present were drinking deep from the cup of this world's pleasure.

CHAPTER III

THE CYCLONE

While the festivities were going forward a great cloud had been silently gathering in the heavens, black as ink, that had closed down all the horizon in utter darkness and shut out every star.

The brilliant lights in the streets, and the multitude of electric lights in the church had so dispersed all gloom that the great, merry throng had not noticed the intense darkness without. The sexton of the church had closed and locked the huge oaken doors from the inside in order to keep out a group of hungry boys of the street who were anxious to at least feast their eyes upon the delicious food within.

There was no thunder and no wind to give warning of the approaching storm that was directly to break with such fury upon the city. The black night without was as still as death. Not a leaf moved or a bird chirped. It seemed as if all nature held her breath in awful suspense, and then with crashing thunderbolts, in leaping lightning, a cyclone burst upon the city.

White Temple Church stood full in its awful path of death. The roof was lifted from the building, the great walls seemed to spring out from each other; the joists supporting the auditorium floor were drawn from their sockets in the walls, and with one tremendous crash the floor fell in upon the shrieking multitude below. Not one escaped. The next moment the swaying, massive walls fell in upon the floor, mashing it down upon the victims beneath with vast tons of weight, and was gone in a few moments, leaving fearful wreck and death behind.

The church was smitten so suddenly that not one of all the multitude within had time for an effort to escape. There were a few moments of wild excitement, a few loud screams for mercy, then the crash of the falling floors, followed by the thunder of the falling walls, and then all was still.

CHAPTER IV

THE ASCENSION

Dr. Star and the members of his church all perished together, and their once captive spirits, now released from the cages of clay, in one united band, all crowding closely together, and all pressing as near to their pastor as possible, commenced their journey heavenward.

It seemed that their souls were as large as their bodies, and they looked much the same. Any one who had known them in the flesh would have experienced no difficulty in recognizing them in the spirit. There was no convoy of angels immediately with them, but in the distance ahead of them, three angels could be seen who were evidently guiding them. One of these angels carried in his hand the large Bible that had for years laid on the pulpit in White Temple Church, and from whose pages Dr. Star had selected the texts from which he had preached to the people. The second angel carried in his hand the church register in which the names of the members of this church were enrolled, and the third angel carried in his hand a great sword which was, in appearance, like a flame of fire. The pastor and his flock followed the ascending angels, swifter than the flight of any bird. Quick as thought they had passed the treetops and gone beyond the highest mountain peaks, and were ascending into the vast heights of the vaulted skies. As the flight continued, the moon was left far beneath the ascending spirits, and, by and by, stars were passed on this side and that some so near that the surface of them could be plainly seen.

A look of anxiety and weariness appeared in the face of Dr. Star, and was fast becoming visible among all those who followed him. Finally, Dr. Star beckons to the angels, and, pointing to a great globe that was floating in the ether not far away, he called out: "Let us stop and rest" At once the angels changed their flight, and turning from their course lighted upon the globe. Sitting down on a mountainside, they beckoned the company to rest in a broad valley which nestled at its feet.

The appearance was much like some of the barren plains of our own great West. There was nothing but a vast waste of sand, no trees or grass or shrubs, except a few stinted, thorny bushes, and a sort of hardy weed. For a time the weary travelers lay very quiet and said but very little, but being somewhat refreshed they began to look about themselves, and to remark on the surroundings. "This is good building stone," said one of the millionaires. "Yes," said an old miner, "In my opinion there is gold in this region. The indicatons are favorable. I should like to prospect here." Meanwhile an old merchant busied himself pulling a handful of the weeds, the stalks of which he broke and twisted, discovering in the weed a fiber, which he declared was so strong and fine that it would make a cloth equal, if not superior, to silk. "If there is plenty of this growth, and it seems to be inexhaustible," said he, "a great factory could be built here, around which a thriving city would soon spring up." "It would be no trouble to build a railroad through this valley if we only had the timber and the iron." said a railroad king, who had been one of the most active men in Dr. Star's congregation. "I have examined the berries of this silkweed," said the president of a large brewing company, who was an official member in White Temple Church, "and I am quite sure if submitted to the proper treatment it would make an excellent drink, if we could get fermentation to take place at this altitude." "There is nothing like trying, papa," said his beautiful daughter.

"Let's build a city here," said a real estate agent, "and improve the place." "How will we fellows get on without our cigarettes," said one of the ushers of the White Temple. "Oh, tobacco may be found here, or a substitute for it," said a stout old merchant.

Dr. Star had been an attentive listener to these remarks, and he said, "On yonder knoll would be an excellent site for a church building, and there is no lack of stone." "Oh, do let's settle here and build a city, and have us a beautiful church, so that we can have entertainments. It would be so nice," chimed in a score of young women at once.

"It all seems so strange to me," said an elderly woman. "I thought when we died we would go to live with the Lord. I don't see him here anywhere." The company engaged in the conversation glanced at each other, and after an awkward pause, one of the sisters said: "Well, we have our dear pastor, he will do." Dr. Star's face, which had been somewhat gloomy, lit up at this compliment, and he bowed his thanks to the sister.

"Well, there is no time to waste," said a nervous young man, "if we are going to do anything let us get at it. I am suffering intensely for a smoke I would give a hundred dollars for a good Havana cigar."

One of the party who seemed to have been a leader, mounted upon a stone, and said: "Fellow-citizens, it will be wise for us to call a convention and set on foot some plans," but just then his speech was cut short by a loud blast from a trumpet, and the three angels on the mountainside arose beckoning the people to follow, which they did, but not without some murmuring.

The reader will notice that these people had in death only changed their place of abode, but their natures remained the same. The same appetites and passions which governed them while in the flesh remained with them when in the spirit. Mark this well. The death of the body does not change the moral character of the soul. Those who expect death to purify their hearts, purge away their sins, and fit them for the enjoyments of heaven, are doomed to disappointment. Death is simply a doorway through which we pass into the spirit world. It does not affect our moral character. Death has no power to pardon or purge away sin. It simply destroys physical life; it does not touch the immortal nature.

After myriads of leagues had been left behind, the trumpet sounded again, and, looking upward, they saw what was evidently heaven, and they were rapidly approaching it. The angels alighted on a broad plain that sloped upward to the crest of a majestic hill, on which the Celestial City stood. Dr. Star and his congregation alighted and followed them. As they were drawing near the city. Dr. Star said to one of his prominent official members, I think the superintendent of his Sunday school, "You lead on, and I will drop back and see if all our people are here."

The Doctor dropped behind, dodged around a little mound, and crept into a rocky cavern in the hillside, and sat down there.

CHAPTER V

STANDING AT HEAVEN'S GATE

As the congregation of the White Temple came near to the city, the great gate of pearl, which was directly before them, swung open, and St. Peter came out and looked at the approaching company, and then took his seat in a large chair at the right-hand side of the gate, while the angel with the sword of flame stood on the left side of the gate, and the other two angels, one with the church register, and the other with the Bible from the pulpit of White Temple, took their stand one on either side of the gate.

The superintendent of the Sabbath school with the people gathered close about him, had by this time come up, and stood before Peter. With some hesitation, he finally said (this man had been a lawyer): "Please, your honor, is this the place of Judgment?" "No," said Peter, "this is neither the time nor place of the general Judment."

Superintendent: "Into what place does this open gateway lead?"

Peter: "It leads into Paradise."

Superintendent: "Are you the gate-keeper?"

Peter: "No, I do not keep the gate. The gate does not need any keeper except the Word of God."

Superintendent "Well, what must we people do?"

Peter: "Who is all this multitude you have here?"

Superintendent: "This is the congregation of White Temple Church, located in the city of——."

Peter: "How does it happen that you all come here together?"

Superintendent: "We were giving an entertainment at our church, and all the membership were present except the children and a few old people of peculiar notions, who think it wrong to give church festivals, and a cyclone struck the church and killed us, as they call it down there. You understand, it broke up our bodies and turned our spirits out of them, and these angels guided us up to this place, and I hope it is the right place for church members, for we are tired. Besides, we have most of us been business men, and we want to get settled down and get at something."

Peter: "Yes, this is the resting place of redeemed souls, walk in and make yourselves at home."

Superintendent: "Well, is there no ceremony or examination of any kind?"

Peter: "No; the time of the judgment is not yet. You are all church members, and, of course are acquainted with the Scriptures. You can judge yourselves, and go in and make yourselves at home."

Superintendent: "I beg your pardon, sir, but we are new comers here, and we do not exactly understand the situation. Can't we get some one to attend to the matter for us?"

At this a great clamor arose among the people, and cries of "no," "no," were heard in every quarter. "Let us all judge ourselves. What better

FROM THE PULPIT TO PERDITION 23

could we ask?" cried many voices at once. "Go on in or get out of the way, and let us in," shouted a number of voices. "I am perishing for water and a smoke," said several at once.

The superintendent saw that the people were displeased with his hesitation, and he said: "Very well, friends, very well; it is all so different from what I thought it would be, that you must excuse me for any blunders I make." And then turning to Peter, who was now intently reading a book which he held in his hand, and addressing him, the superintendent said: "Could you not suggest to us some Scripture by which we may best judge ourselves?"

"Oh, most any text in the Bible," said Peter. "Take, for instance, the inscription over the gate; that will answer your purpose fully."

At this every eye in all the throng was lifted to the arch above the gate, and all read, in great letters of fire: "Without holiness no man shall see the Lord."

For several moments the people stood and gazed in silence without a movement or a word. Then a whispered discussion arose among them as to whether or not the inscription over the gate was a quotation from the Scriptures.

Peter looked up from the pages of his book, and said: "Well, what is the difficulty?"

"I fear the standard is too high," said one. "Well," said Peter, "we have the same standard here that you have down in the world from which you came. I suppose that is fully understood by you all."

"No," answered a gruff old business man, a millionaire, who had made vast sums of money by dealing in tobacco. "No, I did not so understand it. If memory serves me right, our pastor did not believe in this holiness. Indeed, preached against it."

"Where is Dr. Star?" said many voices at once. "Yes, get him. He can fix matters," said one and all.

There was no small stir looking for the pastor. "I know where he is," said a young woman, "I saw him hide among the rocks on the hillside." "Show him to us," said a half dozen strong men, who followed the young woman to the Doctor's hiding place. "Here, what does this mean? We are having trouble up at the gate," said one of the men, in a severe tone. It was a banker who had been one of Dr. Star's greatest admirers.

The Doctor rose up pale and haggard, and crept out of his hiding place, and with a man holding to each arm, he was marched up before Peter, more like a criminal than like a great city pastor.

"Here is the man from whom we learned what we know about the Bible and the future state," said one of them to Peter.

Peter: "You were the pastor of these people, were you?"

Dr. Star: "I was, sir."

Peter: "What did you preach to the people?"

Dr. Star: "The inspired Scriptures."

Peter: "Well, I am not your judge, but your people seemed troubled with the inscription over the gate, and from what I can learn, there seems

FROM THE PULPIT TO PERDITION 25

to have been a mistake made somehow in their instructions."

"I want permission to speak a word here," said the old railroad king. "This man, Star, came to us claiming to be a messenger called and sent by the King of this country. We paid him a large salary, and spent thousands of money on our beautiful Temple. But we were taught by this man, our pastor, that we could not be holy, and it is his duty to see that we are cleared of all blame in the matter."

Peter reached out his hand, and taking the Bible from the angel, said: "What Bible is this?" "That is the Bible that lay on our pulpit in the White Temple," said one.

Peter: "Did you read this book, pastor?"

Dr. Star: "I did."

Peter: "Did you believe it to be an inspired book, and to contain the truths by which men are to be saved?"

Dr. Star: "I did."

Opening the book, Peter placed his fingers under these words, and read them aloud: "Be ye holy, for I, the Lord your God, am holy." "Did you ever see those words?" said Peter, looking at the pastor.

Dr. Star: "Yes, I read them many times."

Peter: "And yet you told the people that they could not be holy."

Dr. Star tried to speak, but his voice was drowned with a great clamor of voices, saying, "Yes, Peter, that is exactly what he did."

Again Peter opened the book, and read: "Thou

shalt call his name Jesus, for he shall save his people from their sins." Peter looked up after a moment's pause, and said: "What did you make out of that, pastor?"

There was the stillness of death. Dr. Star's lips seemed to be sealed.

"He told us," said a society woman, "that that meant we would be saved when we came to die, and it might have turned out all right but you see we all died so suddenly."

"His teachings were false there," said Peter. "Listen to this," and he turned again and read: "The oath which he sware to our father Abraham, that he would grant unto us, that we, being delivered out of the hand of our enemies might serve him without fear, in holiness and righteousness before him all the days of our life."

"Is that in the book out of which Star preached to us?" said the banker. Peter turned the book so that all the people could see the page.

"Star," said the Sabbath school superintendent, "you are a perjured liar." "Let me at him," said a burly fellow who had giggled and flirted in the White Temple choir, and before any one could interfere, he struck the miserable Doctor a blow that felled him to the ground. A fearful scene followed. Some interfered to try to protect their old pastor, and others heaped bitter curses upon his head. Finally order was restored, and Peter again opened the book.

Dr. Star was gotten to his feet, and was supported by a man on either side of him. Looking up at Peter he said, "Please do not read any more from that book." "Read on," said a multitude, "we want to know what it contains."

Peter read: "Wherefore Jesus also, that he might sanctify the people with his own blood, suffered without the gate."

"Hold there, Peter," said a merchant prince, "let me speak a word. Friends, we should be deeply ashamed for what has just occurred here; let's give our pastor a fair chance to clear himself of all blame, if he can do so." Then turning to Dr. Star, he said: "Doctor Star, you well remember when you preached your set of sermons against sanctification—we all remember the time—it was just after the great revival on those lines in our city. Now, I wish to ask you this question: When you preached those sermons were you aware that our Bible contained the Scriptures which Peter has just read?"

Dr. Star remained silent.

"You well remember the sermons," said the merchant; "they came just before that series of sermons you preached to us, in which you explained away all the fire out of hell. You remember how happy we all were over those sermons. Don't you remember that both the president of the brewing company and the president of the jockey club joined our church just after you preached Holiness and Hell out of the Bible? You have not forgotten it. It resulted in a great ingathering to our church. You took in many of the most wealthy and fashionable people in the city into our church just after those sermons, and we increased your salary two thousand dollars. Now, tell me plainly, when preaching those sermons did you know this Scripture, which Peter has just read, was in the Bible?"

"I knew it was there," said the pastor, "but if I had preached it to you, you would not have accepted it, and no doubt would have turned me out to suffer for bread."

"No doubt you will suffer for water hereafter," said a spiteful little woman, whose eyes sparkled with hate.

Again Peter opened the book. "Read on," said a voice from the throng.

"If we walk in the light, as he is in the light, we have fellowship one with another, and the blood of Jesus Christ, his Son, cleanseth us from all sin."

"That will do," roared a voice from the throng. "It is a waste of time to read more. We all know full well that this hireling preached just the opposite of this to us all those years. Chain the deceiver and hand him over to us."

While this investigation was going forward, a company of the less serious and more worldly of the congregation of White Temple had gathered about the gate, and one of the young women, peeping in, said: "What a beautiful place that would be for a lawn fete." "Could a fellow get a box of cigarettes in there?" called out a young man to a passing angel.

"Oh, don't I wish I could pull some of the feathers out of that angel's wing for my summer hat!" said a society leader.

"I will warrant the fruit on yonder tree could be made into hard cider," said a red-faced indi-

FROM THE PULPIT TO PERDITION 29

vidual, who looked about with hungry eyes.

"But don't I wish I could get hold on a few of those yellow paving stones from yonder street," said a young financier.

It would fairly make one's blood run cold to hear them talk. They had brought with them the same depraved nature and appetites that had dominated them in the world below. Had they gotten into Paradise they would have blighted and ruined the place in less than twenty-four hours. It was perfectly plain now, that men must be made heavenly minded before they can enter heaven.

Meanwhile a chain had been brought from a hole in the side of the hill, and a number of men, frantic with anger, were closing about Dr. Star, whose face had taken on more the look of a demon than that of a man. They seized their old pastor, and with many a kick, cuff, and bitter oath, they bound him with a great heavy chain, which seemed glowing red with heat, from which he was never to be released.

Just as the men who had bound Dr. Star completed their task and dragged him to his feet, the great gate of Paradise closed, and the angel with the sword of flame, attended by more than a legion of others, gathered about the company and drove them from the gate toward the foot of a great mountain that could scarcely be outlined in the distance.

For the first time the entire congregation seemed to realize the fearfulness of the situation. Many of them made frantic efforts to escape, but they were caught and chained together like slaves.

Proud women, who had sneered at Holiness, and had mocked at the idea of future punishment, now hung down their heads in speechless horror and shame.

After conducting the people for some distance, the angel handed them over bound to a legion of devils, who came out of the mouth of a great pit that opened at the foot of the mountain. When they finally reached the mouth of the pit, they made a stand, and begged for time for parley and explanation. "We were always taught by our pastor," said one of the people, "that there was no hell, and it seems now that he should bear the blame and we should go free."

"Bring a Bible here," demanded Satan, and it was brought, and turned out to be the same book that had lain on the pulpit at the White Temple Church. "Is this the book from which your pastor preached?" demanded Satan, and the people assented that it was.

"But can we not have some other book opened here? I fear that book," said the wife of a millionaire.

"No," answered Satan, "this is the Book out of which you must be acquitted or condemned." Satan then turned to the following passages and read aloud: "And fear not them which kill the body, but are not able to kill the soul: but rather fear him which is able to destroy both soul and body in hell." He turned again and read: "Cast ye the unprofitable servant into outer darkness; there shall be weeping and gnashing of teeth." Again he turned and read: "And if thy hand offend thee, cut it off; it is better for thee to enter into life maimed than having two hands to go into hell, into the fire that never shall be quenched; where their worm dieth not, and the fire is not quenched." He read still further: "And death and hell were cast into the lake of fire."

By this time the fury of the multitude had become something awful. There was yet one man in the throng who was self-possessed and calm. He had for years been a distinguished criminal lawyer, and of later years, judge on the bench. He had been elected to office by the whiskey element of the district over which he presided. "You need not read more," said the Judge. "Now that it is too late to remedy our sad condition, we shall simply have to face it with as much fortitude as possible. We have pampered and flattered this miserable ecclesiastic for years, and he has deceived us; but we are without excuse. We all see now, as never before, that the Bible is a plainly written book, and easily understood. When Dr. Star first commenced to preach against *holiness*, and to please us with his sermons against the doctrine of hell fire, so plainly taught by Christ, we should at once have recognized him as a wolf in sheep's clothing, seeking our dollars instead of our souls, and should have dismissed him from our pulpit. But, deluded wretches that we were, we loved deception more than we loved the truth."

As the Judge proceeded with these remarks, Dr. Star was crouching close to the ground, and trying to cover his feet with the skirts of his coat, which he could not do, but with his efforts only succeeded in attracting the attention of the people to the fact that both of his feet were cloven, horns shot up from his head, and a great tail, like a serpent, dropped down behind him.

The Doctor uttered a chiek of horror as he beheld himself taking on the image of his diabolical master. Meanwhile the Judge continued his remarks: "The only shadow of a hope of any sort of gratification that I can see left us, is that of haunting and torturing this foul deceiver throughout eternity. It shall be my business to add all I can to his woe and shame."

With this the entire congregation of White Temple Church, with imprecations on their lips, rushed upon their old pastor, and he turned and fled into the mouth of the pit, followed by the people, and in a moment they were all lost to view. As the last one entered the cavern a mighty iron door, with the word ETERNITY written across it, slammed to with such a thunder clap of deafening sound, that I leaped to my feet, thoroughly aroused from the dream-like reverie that had been passing through my mind. But as I dismissed the train of thought, I could but reflect on the vast number of pastors and churches of our times, who seem to be utterly blind and indifferent to the great Bible doctrines of Holiness and Hell.

www.ingramcontent.com/pod-product-compliance
Lightning Source LLC
Chambersburg PA
CBHW030313030426
42337CB00012B/694